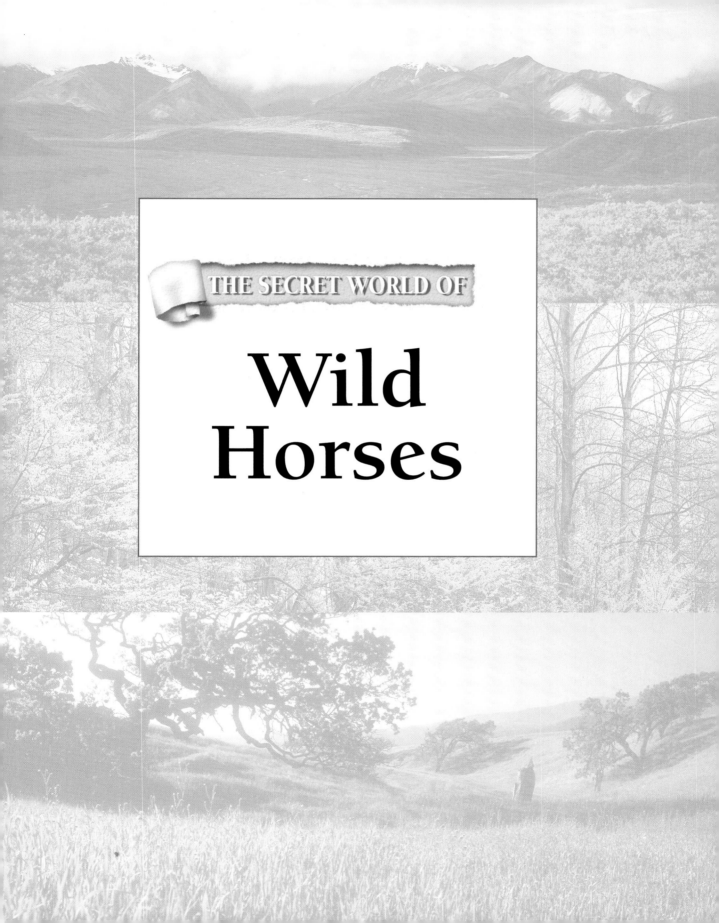

THE SECRET WORLD OF

Wild Horses

THE SECRET WORLD OF

Wild Horses

Malcolm Penny

RAINTREE
STECK-VAUGHN
PUBLISHERS

A Harcourt Company

Austin   New York
www.raintreesteckvaughn.com

Published by Raintree Steck-Vaughn Publishers, an imprint of Steck-Vaughn Company

Acknowledgments
Project Editors: Sean Dolan and Tamsin Osler
Production Manager: Richard Johnson
Consultant: Michael Chinery
Illustrated by Robert Morton
Designed by Ian Winton

Planned and produced by Discovery Books

Library of Congress Cataloging-in-Publication Data
Penny, Malcolm
Wild Horses / Malcolm Penny.
p. cm. -- (Secret world of--)
Includes bibliographical references (p.).
ISBN 0-7398-4987-5

Printed and bound in the United States
1 2 3 4 5 6 7 8 9 LB 05 04 03 02

Contents

CHAPTER 1
Introducing Wild Horses

 A zebra is just what it looks like—a horse with stripes.

 There are 60 million domestic horses in the world, as well as 40 million donkeys and 12 million mules.

 The rarest species of horse is Przewalski's horse, which is native to the deserts of Mongolia. None have been seen in the wild since 1968, and only about 200 survive in captivity.

 Wild horses live for 10 to 25 years; domestic horses can live for 35 years. Wild asses can live up to 40 years.

 The horse known to have lived the longest, "Old Billy," died in England in 1822, at the age of 62.

 Donkeys are domesticated asses descended from the African wild ass.

It seems everybody loves horses. Their beauty, their grace of movement, and their friendship and trusting approach to humans make them many people's favorite animals.

The horses that most people commonly see are domestic horses, which are descended from a single group of wild horses in Asia that began their close association with humans about 6,000 years ago. They have been bred into a wide variety of shapes and sizes for various purposes, including agricultural work, transportation, and recreational use such as horse and chariot racing, polo, and hunting. Smaller varieties of domestic and sporting horses are called ponies. A pony is less than 14.2 hands high at the shoulder. A hand is a unit of measurement used with horses and is equal to 4 inches or 10.2 centimeters.

WILD HORSES TODAY

Wild horses are divided into two main types: true horses, including zebras, which are large and heavily built; and asses, which are smaller and more slender. The home of truly wild horses today is in Africa and across parts of Asia, from the Near East to central Asia and as far north as Mongolia.

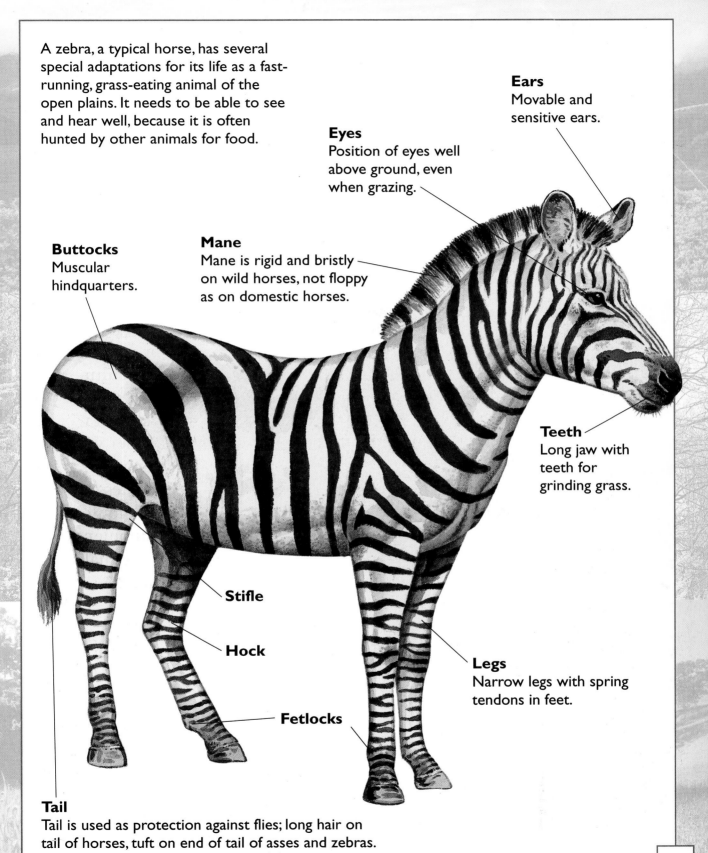

A zebra, a typical horse, has several special adaptations for its life as a fast-running, grass-eating animal of the open plains. It needs to be able to see and hear well, because it is often hunted by other animals for food.

Ears
Movable and sensitive ears.

Eyes
Position of eyes well above ground, even when grazing.

Buttocks
Muscular hindquarters.

Mane
Mane is rigid and bristly on wild horses, not floppy as on domestic horses.

Teeth
Long jaw with teeth for grinding grass.

Stifle

Hock

Legs
Narrow legs with spring tendons in feet.

Fetlocks

Tail
Tail is used as protection against flies; long hair on tail of horses, tuft on end of tail of asses and zebras.

WILD HORSE SPECIES

The oldest surviving species of horse is Grevy's zebra, which for several thousands of years has been confined chiefly to the dry semideserts of Somalia and northern Kenya. It evolved differently from other zebras, and its behavior is more like that of asses than true horses (see Chapter 6). Two other species, the plains zebra and the mountain zebra, evolved later. They are not closely related to Grevy's, though all three live in Africa.

A young domestic horse, sensitive and trusting, arouses protective feelings in most people.

▼ Isolated in the desert, Grevy's zebra developed as a separate species about two million years ago.

There are two main species of wild ass: the African wild ass, which is found in the deserts of the Sahara and in Arabia, and the wild ass of Central Asia.

Somali asses are a subspecies of African ass, adapted to living in harsh, dry conditions.

it is closely related to the domestic horse, the most numerous and varied species of horse.

PRZEWALSKI'S HORSE

The other species of Asian wild horse is Przewalski's horse, which is named for the Russian explorer who discovered it in the 1870s, Nikolai Przewalski. Przewalski's horse no longer exists in the wild and is an endangered species. However,

Przewalski's horse is probably the ancestor of all today's domestic horses.

THE BOLTERS

Although horses were tamed, or domesticated, some 6,000 years ago, their way of life has changed less than other domestic animals such as cows and sheep, and they remain well-suited to living in the wild. This means that when domestic horses escape into the wild, they are able to survive in groups, or herds, as semi-wild or "feral" animals.

Legacy of the Conquistadors

Wild horses were once found all over the Americas, but they were hunted to extinction for food by humans 10,000 years ago. All the horses found in North and South America today, including the mustangs, are descended from those brought by the Spanish conquistadors in the 16th century.

THE MUSTANG

The wild mustangs of North America are descended from horses brought to the continent by European settlers. Their name comes from the Spanish word *mesteños*, which means "strayed" in English. Today mustangs are found mainly in the western states, especially Wyoming, Montana, and Nevada, and in Mexico. In 1999, they numbered more than 40,000. Many Americans are intrigued by the idea that wild horses still roam the mountain pastures of the West, but most ranchers dislike the horses because they compete with their animals for grazing land. Many mustangs end up being slaughtered for use in pet food. To reduce their numbers without killing them,

Mustangs are often seen as the spirit of the Old West, but not everyone loves their wild, untamed beauty.

some are rounded up every year and sold as riding horses.

THE AUSTRALIAN BRUMBY

The feral horses of Australia are known as "brumbies." They are descended from the horses brought to Australia from Europe and the Americas during the Gold Rush of the mid-19th century. Brumbies have adapted so well to the rough and harsh conditions of the Australian outback that they have become too wild to be put to any practical use. Estimated to number about 300,000, they are generally regarded as a pest.

PONIES OF THE BRITISH ISLES

Some ponies live as if they were wild, even though they are owned by people. In England, Dartmoor and Exmoor are the homes of breeds of pony that live freely on the moors all year round. (A moor is an open area of grassy and swampy land.) The moorland ponies are branded to show who owns them, and the young foals are rounded up and auctioned every year.

New Forest ponies in southern England. Like moorland ponies, they live wild all year round.

ICELANDIC PONIES

In Iceland, an island nation in the North Atlantic, about half the ponies live outdoors all year round, even during the hard Icelandic winter. As well as being ridden in races and on cross-country pony treks, they are used as pack and draft animals. The ponies are also killed for meat. They have been a welcome source of food since they were first brought to Iceland in the 9th century by the Viking sailors of Scandinavia.

HORSES OF THE CAMARGUE

Another famous breed of feral horse is the white horse of the Camargue, a region in southern France. Until the end of the 19th century, these 300 square miles (778 sq. km) of marshland and lagoon were home to large herds of wild horses. When people began to drain these wetlands in order to plant grapes and cereals, the horses' habitat was reduced and the herds became smaller. Today these beautiful white horses roam free in the Camargue regional park, which consists of about 200,000 acres (80,937 ha) of protected land.

The Camargue at the mouth of the Rhone River, in southern France, is the home of some of the most beautiful feral horses in the world.

CHAPTER 2
History of the Horse

Horses belong to the same group of animals as the rhinoceros and the tapir, other hoofed mammals with an odd number of toes. Horses began to evolve differently from those animals about 54 million years ago, in the Eocene period. The first horses did not look much like those of today. They were about the size of a small dog.

Malaysia and South America are the home of the tapir, a rare forest animal related to horses. This is a young female tapir.

 The smallest member of the horse family is the African ass, which is native to Sudan, Ethiopia, and Somalia. Its head and body are less than 6 feet (2 m) long, though it can weigh as much as 600 pounds (275 kg), more than the plains and mountain zebra.

Wild asses in Africa and Asia are well-adapted to their environment. They need less water to drink than other horses and can eat and digest the roughest, driest vegetation.

Domestic horses are bred to be slender and graceful; when they revert to the wild, they tend to become more stocky, like wild Przewalski's horses.

Feral horses have a floppy mane, not the stiff, bristly mane found in wild horses. This is a clue to their descent from domestic horses.

THE EVOLUTION OF THE HORSE

In fifty million years, the horse has evolved from a timid forest animal, rather like today's tapirs, into the graceful running animal we know today.

Eohippus

Years ago	50 million

Like the rhinoceros, they had four toes on their front feet and three on the back. Instead of hooves, they had soft pads with thick nails. They lived in the forests that covered most of the Earth at the time, eating fruits and seeds and browsing on the young shoots of shrubs, which grew year-round in the tropical climate of the period.

For 50 million years, most horses lived only in North America. During that time, new species migrated across the land bridge that then connected Alaska and Siberia and spread out across Asia and Europe.

A CHANGE OF CLIMATE

In the Miocene period, some 20 million years ago, the Earth's climate cooled. Away from the Equator, vegetation growth became seasonal and the forests shrank. Areas of grassland appeared in the open spaces where trees used to stand. The open grasslands provided food year-round, and the horses evolved into grassland animals.

As their environment changed, horses evolved in both size and shape. Because they had to run from predators and travel long distances to find food and water, the formerly timid little woodland browsers (called by scientists Eohippus, or "dawn horse") became fast runners on the wide plains. Their legs became longer, and they lost their side toes. They developed hooves. By two million years ago, at the beginning of the Pleistocene period, the horses that we know today had appeared.

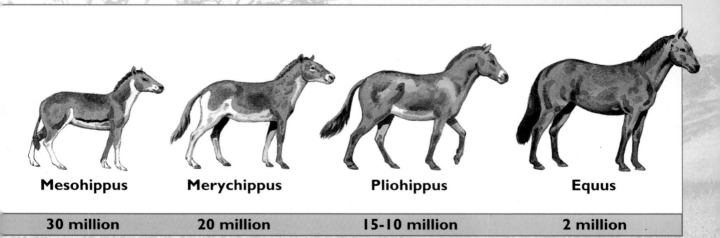

Mesohippus	Merychippus	Pliohippus	Equus
30 million	20 million	15-10 million	2 million

By the end of the last Ice Age, some 10,000 years ago, horses had disappeared from North America. They had been hunted to extinction. The only trace of the horses that had inhabited North America were bones that, one day, would become the fossils, or preserved remains, of ancient animals. These provide modern scientists with clues to the history of the horse.

Horses disappeared from Europe and western Asia but for a different reason. As the Ice Age ended and the climate warmed again, the grasslands where horses lived gave way to forests. The horses migrated eastward to the vast, cool plains of central Asia, leaving behind fossil remains and the drawings of them made by prehistoric humans on the walls of caves. The remains of prehistoric horses have been found on all continents except Australia and

Antarctica. Meanwhile, however, their close relatives thrived on the vast savannas of Africa.

TAMING THE HORSE

The first domestic horses were bred by humans from wild Przewalski's horses about 6,000 years ago. Cave paintings from the Neanderthal period in France and Spain show wild horses that look very similar to Przewalski's horses. The paintings probably date back to the time before climate change forced wild horses to move eastward into Asia.

EARLY RIDERS

The first person to mount and ride a horse was almost certainly a Mongolian herdsman, about 6,000 years ago. The first riders probably

Cave paintings made 13,000 years ago at Lascaux, in France, show small horses that must have been familiar to the people of the time.

Wild Horses of the Himalayas

The Asiatic ass is found in Central and Western Asia, especially Iran, India, and Mongolia. It is also found in Tibet (below). It has been known to western scientists for hundreds of years. In 1995, however, explorers in a high valley in Tibet found wild horses that looked like those in prehistoric cave paintings. They were about four feet tall (1.3 m), with a bristly mane, a black line down their back, and black stripes on their lower legs. They seemed unafraid of people. The explorers learned that local farmers catch the horses with a lasso to use them for riding or to carry loads. Later, the horses are released again. Scientists wonder whether these are feral horses, or whether the explorers witnessed the way wild horses and humans interacted when people first began to domesticate the horse.

did it for fun, racing their half-wild steeds after a day's work. People soon realized that the horse's strength and its friendly nature could make it a valuable assistant in work and an ally in battle.

Careful selective breeding produced the wide range of domestic horses that we know today. The surefootedness of the wild ass led to its domestication at about the same time.

CHAPTER 3
Born to Run

A horse's legs are as long as they can be. If they were any longer, for example, like those of a giraffe, the horse would trip over its own feet when trotting.

Horses can trot at a steady 12 miles per hour (20 kph) for four hours without stopping.

A racehorse galloping at top speed can reach 42 miles per hour (70 kph).

The main cause of death among Asiatic asses in their rocky desert home is broken legs.

All running animals need long, light legs. For its size, the horse has longer legs than most other animals. They are also very light. The lower third of the leg, from the hock (the elevated, backward-bending joint of the hind leg) to the ground, is really the horse's toe, consisting only of bones and tendons, or hard tissue, but no muscles.

A horse runs on the very tip of the toe. "Spring tendons" around the fetlock (the projection just above

A Tunisian Arab gallops his horse across desert sand. The elegant and long-limbed Arab horse is bred for beauty and speed.

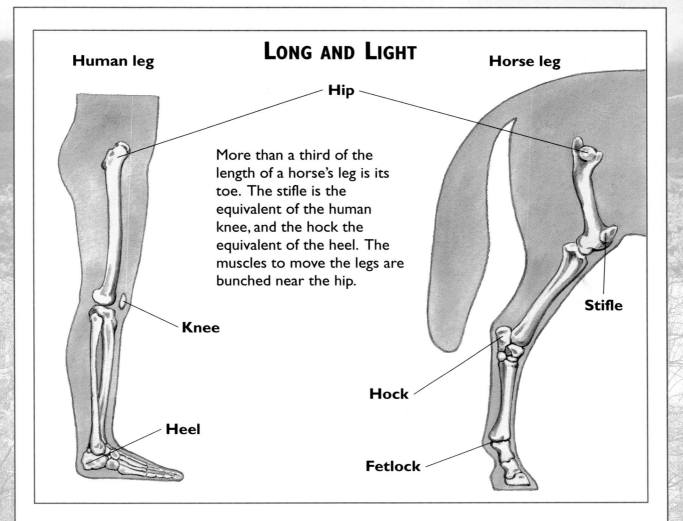

LONG AND LIGHT

Human leg

Horse leg

Hip

More than a third of the length of a horse's leg is its toe. The stifle is the equivalent of the human knee, and the hock the equivalent of the heel. The muscles to move the legs are bunched near the hip.

Knee

Heel

Stifle

Hock

Fetlock

the hoof) act like rubber bands so that when the horse's foot hits the ground, the fetlock bends, absorbing the impact. When the pressure is off that foot, the stretched tendons contract strongly, which helps to lift the foot off the ground, literally giving the horse "a spring in its step."

GIVE A LITTLE, GAIN A LOT
Because their legs are so light and efficient for running, and to save wear on muscles that they do not need, horses do not have some of the movements available to other animals. They cannot rotate their hips, knees, or ankles, for example, as humans can. All these joints are simple hinges moving in one plane only. However, a horse's shoulder blades are not fixed and can slide forward and back, which allows the horse to reach further with each stride of its front legs.

The horse's stifle joint is the equivalent of the human knee. By sliding the kneecap downward, a horse can lock the stifle joint. This means that when a horse is standing still on all four legs, it uses very little energy.

By calculating the amount of energy used by domestic horses, scientists have discovered that they use about 10 percent less energy when they are standing up than they do when lying down. Horses can even sleep standing up.

BREATHE EASY

Horses have big chests as well as big lungs. They also have nostrils that can open wide. This makes their breathing very efficient. A galloping horse breathes once with every stride. The breath is forced out of its lungs when its front feet hit the ground, and air is dragged back in again as it lifts its front feet.

Racehorses are bred to have the longest, slimmest legs of all horses, for added speed.

Disappearing Toes

Horses have only one toe on each foot—the smallest number of any mammal. The reduction in the number of their toes took place when they moved from their original home in woodlands out onto the open plains. To compensate for being so visible in this new environment, they became dependent on increased speed to escape from predators. A one-toed foot is lighter and stronger but still gets a good grip on the ground. The first and fifth toes have disappeared: two bones in the lower leg, known as the splint bones, are the remains of the second and fourth toes, and the third (middle) toe bears the hardened nail that we call the hoof.

FIFTY MILLION YEARS IN THE EVOLUTION OF HORSE'S FEET

Eohippus	Mesohippus	Merychippus	Pliohippus	Equus
50 million years ago	30 million years ago	20 million years ago	15–10 million years ago	2 million years ago

CHAPTER 4
Senses and Behavior

 Zebras watch baboons closely while they are drinking at the same waterhole, because the baboons often give the first warning of danger.

It is believed that foals learn what foods are good to eat by learning the smell of them from their mother's droppings.

Horses' eyes are adapted to see well in poor light, like those of dogs and cats. They have a layer of reflecting cells at the back of the eye, so that incoming light passes twice over the retina—the layer of light-sensitive cells at the back of the eye.

Tests show that horses can recognize red from blue but are unable to distinguish other colors.

The most important senses for the whole horse family are vision and hearing. As prey animals hunted by other animals, horses need to be able to see and hear the danger posed by lions or a pack of hyenas before they get too close. The position of their eyes, high above their long jaws, gives them a better view than other grazing animals with shorter jaws. Even while feeding, their eyes are still as much as 1 foot (30 cm) above the ground.

As this Przewalski's horse grazes, its eyes and ears can look forward and to the side to watch and listen for danger.

DEPTH PERCEPTION

Horses have binocular vision. This helps them to judge distance by looking with both eyes together to get a 3-D effect, although only over a small part of their field of vision. The rest of the field of vision, to the side and rear of the horse, which they see with one eye only, does not produce a sharp image but is very sensitive to movement. This means that a horse has only one small "blind spot," the area behind it, where neither eye can see anything.

The ears of this African wild ass are pointed in different directions as it checks for sounds from in front and behind.

TWITCHING EARS

All horses have highly movable ears that they can turn in the direction of a sound to find out where it is coming from. Like most animals, they hear in stereo: each ear receives slightly different sounds that are interpreted by their brain to help with direction finding. The movement of the ears improves this skill even more.

SNIFFING THE BREEZE

Horses use their sense of smell to detect the approach of predators such as hyenas, wild dogs, and lions. The sense of smell is also important in their social life, especially when they are courting.

THE FLEHMEN REACTION

A mare that is in season, or ready to reproduce, has hormones in her urine that a stallion, or breeding male, can smell. He reacts by opening his mouth and curling his lips back, to pass the smell over a specially sensitive part of the roof of his mouth. This is known as the Flehmen reaction.

CALLING CARDS

Male horses, or "stallions," use their droppings rather as dogs use their urine—depositing a small amount at a time as a signal to other horses. When a stallion finds the droppings of a female horse, or "mare," in season, he smells them, then usually covers them with his own droppings. He may do this to hide the fact that a mare in season

is in the area or as a signal to other males in the group that she is "his," and for them to keep away from her.

Dung transmits other kinds of information, too. Each stallion smells different to other horses. When a horse meets a rival, before they start to fight, they smell each other's droppings so that both will remember the other by his scent. When they meet again, there may be no need to fight because the result will be predictable from the earlier fight.

Stallions also deposit dung in communal piles used by other passing male horses. The communal piles are like a visitors' book, keeping a record of who has passed that way. The dung piles thus contain information about the identity of each passing horse, as well as its status within horse society.

THE OLD WAY

Many animal species use dung piles to mark the boundaries of their territories. Today, most wild

Horse Fights

A full-blown fight between two equally matched stallions is rare, but it can be very fierce and may last for several minutes before one of them gives in. Horses fight with their teeth and hooves. Each tries to bite the other's front legs to cripple him and stop him from giving damaging kicks to the head and face. To defend against this, both fighters often drop to their knees. A stallion also aims bites at his opponent's hindquarters and shoulders. Old, seasoned fighters usually have scars in these places. Fighting is dangerous for both stallions; they avoid it whenever possible.

horses are not territorial, but some people suggest that this habit of making dung piles is left over from a time when they were. The only wild horses that are territorial are Grevy's zebra and the African wild ass, both thought to be relatively primitive kinds of horse. Sure enough, both species mark their boundaries with piles of dung.

CHAPTER 5
Food and Feeding

The black rhino is the only relative of the horse that is a browser—eating leaves from trees and bushes—not a grazing animal.

Horses spend at least 60 percent of the day and night eating. This can rise to 80 percent when food is harder to find.

Horses often chew small quantities of some kinds of soil for the salts and minerals they contain.

The age of a horse can be judged by checking the wear on its teeth from chewing grass.

Judging from their fossil teeth, the first horse-like animals probably lived for only 4 years.

The horse's ancestors in the forest fed mainly on fresh shoots. But they also ate fruits and seeds, which are rich foods and easy to digest. As horses evolved into bigger animals, it became harder for them to satisfy their appetite. The easiest food to find, and the main diet of all large hoofed animals, is grass.

Although grass is abundant, it has one main drawback: it is tough. So horses' teeth had to change to cope with it. From having flat chewing surfaces, the back teeth of horses evolved complicated ridges of enamel—the hard substance that

HORSE TEETH

Incisors, the sharp front teeth, crop the grass, and molars, the massive back teeth, grind it up for digestion. The curved canine teeth are very small, since a horse does not need to rip open the flesh of prey animals.

Incisors

Molars

Canines

The simple molar surfaces of ancient woodland horses' teeth evolved into the complex grinding patterns of modern horses.

covers teeth—suitable for grinding up tough grass stems. The front teeth are used for biting and cropping shorter grass.

HELPFUL BACTERIA

Grass is also difficult to digest, so their digestive system had to change, too. How can large animals survive on food that they cannot digest? The answer is that horses depend on a little extra assistance for digestion. Their food is actually broken down into a form that they can use by bacteria, tiny single-celled organisms that live inside their digestive canals. This process is called fermentation. To allow their food to ferment, herbivores, or grass-eating animals, need a large chamber where the food can be held while the bacteria do their work.

▲ Zebras join wildebeest on their annual migration across the African plains. The grasses of the plains provide the animals with the food they need.

A donkey, the domestic form of ass, has a varied diet. Here, it is surrounded by lush, fresh vegetation, but it can eat much coarser plants, even thistles.

ROUGH AND READY

Horses, and their relatives the rhinoceros and the tapir, ferment their food in the cecum, a large bag between the small and large intestines. They pack the cecum full of grass, and wait for the bacteria to break it down. They do not wait very long, however. Food passes through a horse in 48 hours, compared to the 70 to 90 hours it takes food to pass through a cow.

I DIDN'T KNOW THAT

Eating and Drinking Companions

On the African plains, zebras and wildebeest often feed together. The wildebeest eat the leaves of grasses, while zebras crunch up the rough stems. They often drink at the same waterhole, too.

A horse extracts only seven-tenths as much energy from its food as a cow, but it does so quickly. By processing larger amounts of food, it can gather the same total amount of energy. In order to collect enough food to be processed in this rather inefficient way, horses often feed during the night as well as during the day.

Camargue horses often browse from trees and brushes, because the grass in their marshy habitat can be too salty for them.

Horses can browse as well as graze, eating leaves, buds, fruits, and even roots. Asses, especially the domestic asses known as donkeys, are famous for being able to eat almost anything.

29

CHAPTER 6
Horse Lifestyles

 Before horses were used for riding, they were hunted and later bred in captivity for food.

 Horses need companionship. If no other horses are around, they will make friends with other animals—cats, dogs, or humans.

 Stallions sometimes mark their boundaries by brushing against bushes to leave their scent for other horses to find.

 Scratching a domestic horse's neck calms it down, because it imitates the way wild horses groom each other.

All horses are highly social animals, living together in cooperative herds or bands. Their behavior is peaceful throughout most of the year. What little conflict there is usually happens during the breeding season, when males compete for mates from among the females in the herd.

FAMILY PARTIES

There are two forms of social organization among wild horses. The more common form is found among both the plains zebra and the mountain zebra, Przewalski's horse, and feral domestic horses. They live in herds, in which a senior stallion controls a group, or harem, of three or four mares. Typically, each mare will have a young foal with her. The rest of the herd will be made up of colts, or

After the breeding season, herds of horses often join together to feed. These herds are in the Dolmen swampland, in northwest Germany.

These Icelandic ponies are grooming each other. This helps to remove skin parasites, but also reinforces social bonds between members of a herd.

Although home ranges often overlap, the stallions usually avoid meeting to reduce the chance of having to fight. The ranges may shift with the seasons as the herds move to find the best grazing. The size of the range depends on the quality of the food available. Where the grazing is good, the home range is smaller.

Plains zebras in the rich pastures of the Ngorongoro crater in Tanzania, Africa, hold home ranges varying from 30 to 100 square miles (80 to 250 sq. km). Ranges in the Serengeti National Park, also in Tanzania, even during the rainy season from March to May, may be as large as 135 square miles (350 sq. km). When the dry season comes, the Serengeti bands join together and move to better grazing as much as 60 miles (100 km) away. There, when they spread out again, the home ranges may be as big as 230 square miles (600 sq. km).

yearling males, tolerated by the stallion until they grow big enough to offer a threat to his authority, and fillies, young females that have not yet been kidnapped by males from outside the herd (see page 34).

The mares generally maintain friendly relations among themselves, grooming each other and standing together in groups. However, some mares are senior to others, and they and their foals have first access to water when it is scarce as well as to the best food.

ROOM TO FEED

Each stallion, with his harem, holds a home range. This is different from a territory in that it does not exclude other horses.

A LONELY LIFE

Grevy's zebras, together with the Asian and African asses, have a different social organization. Most adult males hold large individual territories from which all other adult males are kept out. They mark their boundaries with piles of dung. These territories may be as large as 4 square miles (10 sq. km) for Grevy's zebras, and nearly 6 square miles (15 sq. km) for the asses.

Females passing through the

An onager, a type of Asian wild ass, leads a lonely life in its desert home, where food is usually scarce and hard to find.

territory, if they are in heat, will become the mates of the resident male, and stay with him while they have their young. The rest of the adult population move around in temporary groups, usually of the same sex, but sometimes mixed. When the males in these groups are old and strong enough, they set up and defend territories of their own, but until then they cannot mate.

The lonely life of these horses is forced on them by the shortage of food. In the deserts where they live, food is poor and scarce so each horse must fend for itself. Large herds would only fight over what little food they could find, so harems are out of the question. Rather than defending harems, these males have to set up and defend areas where females must come if they want to feed.

SIGNS AND SIGNALS

Being naturally highly sociable animals, horses have a wide range of signals to indicate their mood to each other. As well as threatening with flattened ears and lowered head, they have a range of body language to indicate other moods. The swing of a head or the raising of a hoof may seem insignificant to us, but they are strong forms of horse communication.

Horses use a range of sounds, too. Young foals click their teeth to show that they submit to an adult. Adults have a variety of snickers, whinnies, squeals, and blows with which they "speak" to each other. Unfortunately, we can only guess what they actually mean.

Horse Talk

I DIDN'T KNOW THAT

Horses recognize the voices of horses that they know, just as humans know the voices of family, friends, and acquaintances. Mares respond more often to the whinny of their own foal than to that of other foals, and adult feral horses will reply only to the whinny of one of their own band. These sounds can carry for more than a quarter of a mile (400 m).

CHAPTER 7
Reproduction

Grevy's zebras are pregnant for longer than other wild horses. Their gestation period is just over a year (390 days).

Males chase females in a characteristic posture, with their head down and their ears laid back.

In temperate climates the mating season lasts from early spring into summer.

Once their harem (group of mares) is established, stallions do not usually try to kidnap more females.

Young female horses live with the herd into which they were born until they become sexually mature at about two years old. Then they leave with a male who has "kidnapped" them by chasing them away from their own herd. This may sometimes be the leading male of a nearby herd, but it is more often a bachelor who is starting his own herd. Bachelor groups form when males of about four years old are finally forced to leave their own herd, because they have become a threat to the leading stallion.

When a new stallion takes over a zebra herd, he drives away the foals of the previous stallion. (A white rhino blunders away from the disturbance.)

A stallion keeps a close watch on one of his mares as she gives birth.

These bachelor groups are like a training school for the young males, where they spend a few years growing strong and learning how to fight, so that they can defend a territory of their own. The fights often look very fierce, but they are usually just sparring sessions in which each horse avoids hurting the other, rather like karate practice. The sparring usually ends with the two horses standing or trotting peacefully side by side.

THE MATING SEASON

Mating takes place after the rainy season in Africa, or in spring to summer elsewhere, when the grass is growing at its best, and there is plenty of food. The mare gives birth about a year later, almost always having only one foal. Horses give birth lying on their side, with the stallion standing guard close by. The foal is on its feet and feeding from its mother within an hour of being born. This is important, because it must be able to travel with the herd if the need arises.

Less than an hour after it is born, a foal can feed from its mother.

Foals weigh about 65 to 80 pounds (30 to 36 kg), males being slightly heavier. They are usually the same color as they will be in adulthood, but with thick fluffy hair that helps to keep them warm while they are small. Zebra foals have brown stripes instead of black: they change to the adult color when the foal is about four months old.

KEEP AWAY

For the first few days after the birth, the mother chases away any horse that comes too close to her foal, including its father. This is not so much because she is afraid that her foal might be hurt, but to make sure that imprinting occurs properly, with herself identified as the foal's mother.

Imprinting is a special type of learning that is very important for the foal. Animals that live close to their mothers for a time after they are born learn to recognize her because she is the only thing in their world. But animals that must be able to run, often for their lives, soon after being born need another way of remembering who she is. For the first crucial few days of its life, the foal will accept as its mother the first moving thing it sees. Once imprinting is complete, the mother lets the foal join the herd.

Young zebras often pretend to fight together in play.

GROWING UP

The foal grows quickly, putting on about one pound (0.5 kg) per day for the first two months of its life. It is a playful little creature, chasing and racing with other foals of its own age in the herd, or if it is a male, staging mock fights with other young males. They may even play with animals of different species: zebra foals in Africa have been seen playing with young wildebeest and gazelle calves while their mothers graze together nearby.

A mare and foal running together. A foal is seldom far from its mother's side.

Foals begin grazing for themselves within a few weeks, but they are not properly weaned until they are between 8 and 13 months old. They return constantly to their mother's side, to feed and to be groomed by her. Their life is pleasant, but it might be quite short. Depending on the weather and how much food is available, and on the pressure from predators, between 30 and 60 percent of foals die in their first few months.

Although mares are ready to mate again within seven to ten days after their foal is born, most skip a season while they bring up a foal, giving birth again only when their foal is nearly ready to look after itself. Some species of horse are ready to mate again every 21 days until the end of the breeding season, for as long as food supplies last.

Mares' Milk

Some breeds of horse, such as the Bashkir and the Kazakh (below) of the central Russian steppes, are kept for their meat and their milk, as well as for use as draft animals and for sporting activities. The Bashkir, which is domesticated now, was once a distinct wild race of horse. In the eight months while she raises a foal, a Bashkir mare produces some 500 gallons (1600 liters) of milk. Its curly winter coat, brushed out in spring, is used to weave into cloth.

I DIDN'T KNOW THAT

CHAPTER 8
Threats and Conservation

Races, or subspecies, of wild horse found in Asia include wild asses, known as the kulan of Mongolia, the kiang of Nepal, Tibet, and Sikkim, and the onager in Iran.

The quagga, a yellowish-brown zebra with stripes only on its head, found in South Africa, was made extinct in the 1880s. It was hunted for its meat and skin.

In Kazakhstan domestic horses are bred for meat and milk. The meat is called "qazy," and the milk is fermented to make an alcoholic drink called "qymyz," or "koumiss" in Russian.

When the warrior Ghengis Khan crossed the Gobi desert to raid cities in China, his soldiers survived by drinking mares' milk and the blood of their horses.

Horses have been hunted for thousands of years. We have already seen how they were wiped out by native hunters in North America after the Ice Age. Evidence from a site in Ukraine shows that people there were hunting them for meat long before they were first domesticated 6,000 years ago.

Elsewhere, wild horses were killed to prevent them from mating with domestic horses and so spoiling

One subspecies of Asiatic ass, the onager, has become very rare in the deserts of Iran. However, a captive population set up in Israel has bred well enough for some of them to be released into the desert there, where they are doing very well.

generations of breeding by humans. This was the main reason for the extermination of African and Asiatic asses over large parts of the Middle East and North Africa. In some agricultural areas in Africa, zebras were killed because they ate crop plants, and invaded pasture that ranchers wanted for their cattle.

HORSES IN DANGER

Today, the African ass, Grevy's zebra, and Przewalski's horse are listed as endangered species. The Asiatic ass and the mountain zebra are classed as vulnerable, or under threat. Przewalski's horse was common in Mongolia, Kazakhstan, and parts of China until the late 19th century, but by the beginning of the 20th century, it was under pressure from nomadic cattle rearers as they tried to protect water sources and grazing for their stock. It was last seen in the wild in 1968. Only about two hundred now survive in captivity.

A SHAMEFUL TRADE

The reason for the sad state of two of the three species of zebra is partly hunting to protect farmland,

A Przewalski's horse in a Scottish wildlife park. The cave-painters made the head a bit small (see p. 16), but the shape and color are very accurate.

and partly shooting for skins and souvenirs. Even very recently, African tourist shops sold rugs, drums, and clothing made from zebra skins. This trade is now banned by international agreement, but the zebras are slow to recover because their habitat is in great demand for farming and because their breeding rate is so slow. A mare gives birth to only one foal at a time.

41

RETURN OF THE TARPAN

There was once a wide range of wild horses in Europe. While they were not exactly domesticated, they were not completely wild, because all of them were used to some extent by humans for carrying or for riding. The last of them were small greyish horses with a flowing mane and tail, descendants of the tarpan of eastern Europe and Russia. In the 19th century, the tarpan were hunted for raiding crops, and by the turn of the century, they were extinct.

In some places before then, though, tarpans had interbred with domestic horses. In Munich Zoo,

A family of tarpan-like horses grooming each other, with the foal joining in. The floppy mane reveals that they are not truly wild horses, but bred back from tarpans crossed with domestic horses.

Zebroids and Other Hybrids

Horses, zebras, and asses can all interbreed. A mule is a cross between a female horse and a male donkey, or jackass. A hinny, or jennet, is a cross between a male horse and a female donkey, or jenny. A zebroid (below) is the product of a horse and a zebra, and a shebra the product of a Shetland pony and a zebra. The fact that they can interbreed so efficiently is evidence that all species of horse are closely related.

in Germany, horses with visible tarpan features were carefully bred to try to "recreate" the race. These tarpan-like horses are on show in zoos and collections in Europe and North America. Because they can live on very poor pasture, they are sometimes used to control rough grassland in several European countries.

Glossary

BROWSER – an animal that eats leaves from bushes and trees

CANTERING – running with front and hind feet moving as pairs, a slow gallop

COLT – male horse under four years old

DOMESTIC – under the management and control of humans

DRAFT – The term applied to horses that are used for pulling carts and other vehicles

EVOLVE – to change gradually over a long period

EXTINCT – no longer alive anywhere on Earth

FERAL – having run wild, after once being domesticated

FILLY – female horse under four years old

GALLOPING – running so that all four feet are off the ground at each stride

HAREM – a group of mares (females) kept together for breeding purposes by a male stallion

HERBIVORE – an animal that eats only plants and other vegetation

HORMONES – Chemical substances in the body that control life-processes such as growth and reproduction

MARE – a female horse capable of breeding

PREY – an animal that is regularly eaten by other animals

SAVANNA – open grassland with scattered trees

SPECIES – a kind or type of animal

STALLION – a male horse capable of reproducing

TROTTING – walking with front and hind legs moving separately, not together as in cantering and galloping

TROPICAL – hot and humid, like the climate near the equator today

WEAN – To progress from no longer being dependent on the mother's milk

Further Reading

Henry, Marguerite. *Album of Horses*. New York: Simon & Schuster Children's Books, 1993.

Miller, Sara Swan. *Horses and Rhinos: What They Have in Common*. Danbury, CT: Franklin Watts Inc., 2000.

Viola, Herman J. *After Columbus: The Horse's Return to America*. Norwalk, CT: Soundprints, 1992.

Wilcox, Charlotte. *The Tennessee Walking Horse (Learning About Horses)*. Mankato, MN: Capstone Press, 1996.

Acknowledgments

Front cover: Robert Maier/Bruce Coleman Collection; p.8t: Chris Fairclough/Discovery Picture Library; p.8b: Bruce Coleman Collection; p.9t: E. & D. Hosking/Frank Lane Picture Agency; p.9b: Terry Whittaker/FLPA; p.10: Duncan Maxwell/Robert Harding Picture Library; p.11: Bruce Coleman Collection; p.12: Derek Middleton/FLPA; p.13: Christophe Ratier/Natural History Photographic Agency; p.14: Rod Williams/Bruce Coleman Collection; p.16: RHPA; p.17: Minden Pictures/FLPA; p.18: Capel/Sunset/FLPA; 20: M. Clark/FLPA; p.22: Andy Rouse/NHPA; p.23: E.A. Janes/NHPA; p.25: Sarah Cook/Bruce Coleman Collection; p.27t: Bruce Coleman Collection; p.27b: Susanne Danegger/NHPA; p.28: Konrad Wothe/Oxford Scientific Films; p.29: Henry Ausloos/NHPA; p.30: M. Kwias/FLPA; p.31: W. Wisniewski/FLPA; p.32: Bruce Coleman Collection; p.33: Martin Withers/FLPA; p.34: Nigel J. Dennis/NHPA; p.35: E. Schmale/FLPA; p.36: Bruce Coleman Collection; p.37: Tim Jackson/OSF; p.38: Bruce Coleman Collection; p.39: Sarah Errington/Hutchinson Picture Library; p.40: Steven C. Kaufman/Bruce Coleman Collection; p.41: William S. Paton/Bruce Coleman Collection; p.42: Rolf Bender/FLPA; p.43: Frank W. Lane/FLP;. All background images © Steck-Vaughn Collection (Corbis Royalty Free, Getty Royalty Free, and StockBYTE).

Index

Numbers in *italic* indicate pictures